Also by Aurelia Peries

Cancer and Chemotherapy

Coping with Cancer & Chemotherapy Treatment: What You Need to Know to Get Through Chemo Sessions

Coping with Cancer: How Can You Help Someone with Cancer, Dealing with Cancer Family Member, Facing Cancer Alone, Dealing with Terminal Cancer Diagnosis, Chemotherapy Treatment & Recovery

Chemotherapy Survival Guide: Coping with Cancer & Chemotherapy Treatment Side Effects

Chemotherapy Chemo Side Effects And The Holistic Approach: Alternative, Complementary And Supplementary Proven Treatments Guide For Cancer Patients

Chemotherapy Treatment: Comforting Gift Book For Patients Coping With Cancer

Christian Books

Seeking Salvation, Secure In Belief: How To Get Sure-Fire Saved By Grace Through Faith, Rapture Ready And Heaven Bound

Thriving In Chaos: A Practical Guide To Surviving In A World Of Uncertainty: Strategies and Tools for Building Resilience, Finding Stability, and Flourishing in Turbulent Times

Divine Mathematics: Unveiling the Secrets of Gematria Exploring the Mystical & Symbolic Significance of Numerology in Jewish and Christian Traditions, & Beyond

Eating At Night Time: Sleep Disorders, Health and Hunger Pangs: Tips On What You Can Do About It

Addiction To Food: Proven Help For Overcoming Binge Eating Compulsion And Dependence

Weight Loss: How To Not Gain Holiday Weight After Thanks Giving & Christmas Holidays Beat Post Vacation Weight Gain: Proven Ways To Jumpstart Healthy Eating

Weight Loss After Having A Baby: How To Lose Postpartum Weight After Pregnancy & Giving Birth

Food Addiction And Emotional Eating Guidebook: Proven Ways To End Binge Eating, Sugar Cravings & Eating At Night-Time

Eating Disorders: Food Addiction & Its Effects, What Can You Do If You Can't Stop Overeating?

Slim Down Sensibly: A Realistic Guide to Achieving Sustainable Weight Loss A Science-Based Approach to Healthy Eating, Exercise, and Mindset for Lasting Results

Eye Care
Glaucoma Signs And Symptoms

Food Addiction
Overcoming Food Addiction to Sugar, Junk Food. Stop Binge Eating and Bad Emotional Eating Habits

Food Addiction: Overcoming Emotional Eating, Binge Eating and Night Eating Syndrome

Weight Loss Without Dieting: 21 Easy Ways To Lose Weight Naturally
Weight Loss Affirmations For Food Addicts: You Can Do It Believe In Yourself Daily Positive Affirmations To Help You Lose Weight

Grief, Bereavement, Death, Loss
Coping with Loss & Dealing with Grief: Surviving Bereavement, Healing & Recovery After the Death of a Loved One
How to Plan a Funeral
Coping With Grief And Heartache Of Losing A Pet: Loss Of A Beloved Furry Companion: Easing The Pain For Those Affected By Animal Bereavement
Grieving The Loss Of Your Baby: Coping With The Devastation Shock And Heartbreak Of Losing A Child Through Miscarriage, Still Birth
Loss And Grief: Treatment And Discovery Understanding Bereavement, Moving On From Heartbreak And Despair To Recovery
Grief: The Grieving Process, Reactions, Stages Of Grief, Risks, Other Losses And Recovery
First Steps In The Process Of Dealing With Grief: Help for Grieving People: A Guidebook for Coping with Loss. Pain, Heartbreak and Sadness That Won't Go Away

Health Fitness

How To Avoid Colds and Flu Everyday Tips to Prevent or Lessen The Impact of Viruses During Winter Season

Boost Your Immune System Fast: Guide On Proven Ways For Boosting Your Immunity Against Illness And Disease.

International Cooking

Spicy Seafood Dishes: Gourmet Cooking Ideas For Curry And Spice Lovers. Introductory Guide To Decadent Seafood Cuisine With Health Benefits & Wellbeing For The Connoisseur

Noodles: Noodle Recipes Introductory Guide To Delicious Spicy Cuisine International Asian Cooking

A Taste Of Malaysia: Authentic Recipes For Nasi Lemak, Satay, Laksa, And More: Unveiling The Secrets Of Malaysian Cuisine Through Delicious And Easy-to-Follow Dishes

Discovering the Flavours and Traditions of Burma (Myanmar): A Guide to Burmese Cuisine and Culture A Journey Through Food, Fashion, Art and History

Parenting

Anger Management For Stressed-Out Parents:Skills To Help You Cope Better With Your Child

Coding Programs For Kids: Parents Guidebook: How Your Child Can Learn To Code And The Benefits For Their Future

Compassionate Collaborative Communication: How To Communicate Peacefully In A Nonviolent Way A Practical

Guide Using Effective Proven Skills For Conflict In Relationships Between Parents & Kids
Potty Training: Handbook Guide In Crap Parenting Proven Ways To Train Your Toddler Easily & Quickly With Realistic Results
Acts Of Kindness: Doing Good Deeds to Help Others

Personal Relationships
How To Talk To Your Partner: Preventing Problems Through Effective Communication In A Relationship

Quark Cheese
50 More Ways to Use Quark Low-fat Soft Cheese: The Natural Alternative When Cooking Classic Meals
Quark Cheese Recipes: 21 Delicious Breakfast Smoothie Ideas Using Quark Cheese
30 Healthy Ways to Use Quark Low-fat Soft Cheese
Introduction To Quark Cheese And 25 Recipe Suggestions: Quark Cheese Guide And Recipes

Quit Alcohol
How To Stop Drinking Alcohol: Coping With Alcoholism, Signs, Symptoms, Proven Treatment And Recovery

Relationships
The Grief Of Getting Over A Relationship Breakup: How To Accept Breaking Up With Your Ex | Advice And Tips To Move On
Coping With A Marriage Breakup: How To Get Over The Emotional Heartbreak Of A Relationship Breakdown, Signs Of Splitting Up, Divorce And Heal From A Broken Heart

Self Help
OCD: Introduction Guide Book Obsessive Compulsive Disorder And How To Recover

Sleep Disorders
Sleep Better at Night and Cure Insomnia Especially When Stressed

Standalone
Family Style Asian Cookbook: Authentic Eurasian Recipes: Traditional Anglo-Burmese & Anglo-Indian
Coping with Loss and Dealing with Grief: The Stages of Grief and 20 Simple Ways on How to Get Through the Bad Days
Coping With Grief Of A Loved One After A Suicide: Grieving The Devastation And Loss Of Someone Who Took Their Own Life. How Long Does The Heartache Last?

When A Person Goes Missing And Cannot Be Found: Coping With The Grief And Devastation, Without Losing Hope, Of When An Adult Or Child Disappears

Menopause For Women: Signs Symptoms And Treatments A Simple Guide

Remembering Me: Discover Your Memory Proven Ways To Expand & Increase It As You Get Older

Boredom: How To Overcome Feeling Bored Discover Over 100 Proven Ways To Beat Apathy

Putting Baby To Sleep: Soothe Your Newborn Baby To Sleep For Longer Stretches At Night Proven Practical Survival Guide For Tired Busy New Parents

Coping With Bullying And Cyberbullying: What Parents, Teachers, Office Managers, And Spouses Need To Know: How To Identify, Deal With And Cope With A Bully At Home, In School Or In The Workplace

Gardening For Beginners: How To Improve Mental Health, Happiness And Well Being Outdoors In The Garden: Green Finger Holistic Approach In Nature: Everything You Need To Know, Even If You Know Nothing!

Becoming Vegan For Health And The Environment: Plant Based Veganism Guidebook For Beginners: Balanced View Of The Benefits & Risks Of Being Vegetarian

Happiness & Reading Books: For Adults & Children A Proven Way To Increase Literacy Focus Improve Memory Sleep Better Relieve Stress Broaden Your Knowledge Increase Confidence Motivation & Be Happy

Caring For A Loved One With Cancer & Chemotherapy Treatment: An Easy Guide for Caregivers

Genealogy Tracing Your Roots A Comprehensive Guide To Family History Research Uncovering Your Ancestry, Building Your Family Tree And Preserving Your Heritage

Table of Contents

Divine Mathematics: Unveiling the Secrets of Gematria

Exploring the Mystical & Symbolic Significance of Numerology in Jewish and Christian Traditions, & Beyond

Anthea Peries

I. Introduction

For ages, gematria, the practice of assigning numerical values to Hebrew letters, has enthralled and divided people.

For some, it is a potent instrument for deciphering the hidden meanings of ancient books, discovering the world's secrets, and even predicting the future.

For others, it is a mere superstition or a dangerous distraction from the true spiritual path.

In "*Divine Mathematics: Unveiling the Secrets of Gematria*," we will explore the history, principles, and applications of Gematria in Jewish and Christian traditions, as well as in other cultures around the world.

We will examine numerology's mystical and symbolic significance and how it has been used to deepen our understanding of the divine realm.

We will review familiar stories from the Hebrew Bible and the New Testament through the lens of gematria, looking for hidden patterns and connections that may have evaded us previously.

We'll look at how gematria has been utilised to understand sacred texts, direct meditation, and inspire devotion in Kabbalah, Christian mysticism, and other spiritual traditions.

We'll also look at the controversies over gematria, from sceptics who dismiss it as mere numerology to religious leaders who have outlawed or discouraged its usage.

Finally, we will look at theological discussions about the proper use of Gematria in Christian apologetics and the ethical quandaries raised by its use in divination and other forms of spiritual practice.

Finally, we will discuss the present significance of gematria and its implications for our understanding of spirituality, numerology, and mathematics.

"Divine Mathematics" invites you to discover the power and beauty of gematria and unearth the hidden secrets of the divine realm, whether you are a scholar, a spiritual seeker, or simply interested in the mysteries of the universe.

Definition Of Gematria

———

The technique of assigning numerical values to letters of an alphabet to discover hidden meanings or connections between words and phrases is known as gematria.

It is usually linked with the Hebrew alphabet, but it can also be used in other alphabets and languages.

In Jewish and Christian mystical traditions, gematria is frequently employed to interpret and comprehend sacred texts as well as other spiritual and occult practices.

Brief History Of Gematria

———

The roots of gematria are unknown; however, it is thought to have originated in the Jewish community of ancient Palestine during the Second Temple period (516 BCE to 70 CE).

Some experts believe it was influenced by Greek or Egyptian numerology, while others believe it is entirely Jewish.

The Hebrew Bible, however, has the oldest known example of gematria, in which the numerical value of specific words and phrases is utilised to communicate symbolic or mystical significance.

Gematria gained popularity in the Jewish mystical tradition of Kabbalah during the Middle Ages, particularly in the 13th century, with the publication of the "*Sefer Yetzirah*," a foundational Kabbalistic text.

Gematria was utilised in Kabbalistic interpretations of the Torah to discover hidden levels of significance and disclose the universe's mysterious secrets.

Gematria was very important in the early Christian tradition, especially in the writings of the Church Fathers and the creation of Christian numerology.

Furthermore, some Christian theologians employed gematria to argue for Jesus' divinity and to interpret prophetic scriptures from the Old and New Testaments.

Gematria has captivated scholars, mystics, and occultists of numerous traditions in the contemporary period. It has been used in various domains, including cryptography, numerology, and the study of ancient languages.

Purpose Of This Book

———

T he goal of "Divine Mathematics: Unveiling the Secrets of Gematria" is to present a comprehensive review of gematria practice, including its history, concepts, and applications in Jewish and Christian traditions, as well as other civilisations around the world.

The book aims to provide readers with a deeper understanding of the mystical and symbolic significance of numerology and how it has been used to interpret sacred texts, guide meditation, and inspire devotion.

The book also addresses the controversies and ethical considerations surrounding gematria, examining the theological debates over its proper use in Christian apologetics and the ethical dilemmas posed by its application in divination and other forms of spiritual practice.

Finally, the book challenges readers to evaluate the significance of gematria in our modern world and its implications for our understanding of spirituality, numerology, and mathematics.

By giving a balanced and comprehensive investigation of gematria, the book intends to increase our appreciation for this ancient technique and inspire new insights and understandings.

II. Mathematical Principles of Gematria

———

Hebrew letters are allocated numerical values. Each letter of the Hebrew alphabet is assigned a number value in gematria.

The Hebrew numerals are a system for assigning numerical values to letters.

Here are the numerical values assigned to the 22 letters of the Hebrew alphabet:

Aleph (1 = (א

Bet (2 = (ב

Gimel (3 = (ג

Dalet (4 = (ד

Hei (5 = (ה

Vav (6 = (ו

Zayin (7 = (ז

Het (8 = (ח

Tet (9 = (ט

Yod (10 = (י

Kaf (20 = (כ

Lamed (30 = (ל

Mem (40 = (מ

Nun (50 = (נ

Samekh (60 = (ס

Ayin (70 = (ע

Pei (80 = (פ

Tsadei (90 = צ)

Qof (100 = ק)

Resh (200 = ר)

Shin (300 = ש)

Tav (400 = ת)

The numerical value of a word or phrase is calculated by summing the numerical values of its constituent letters.

For example, the word "*chai*," which means "*life*" in Hebrew, has a numerical value of 18 (8+10).

First, we look up the numerical value of each letter in the word:

Chet (8 = ח)

Yod (10 = י)

Next, we add the numerical values of the letters together:

8 + 10 = 18

So the numerical value of the word "*chai*" is 18.

This same process can be applied to longer words and even entire phrases.

The resulting numerical value, according to gematria practitioners, can disclose hidden meanings or links between words and concepts and provide insights into the spiritual or mystical significance of the word or phrase.

Basic Operations of Gematria

———

Gematria's fundamental operations entail assigning numerical values to the letters of a word or phrase and then conducting mathematical operations on those values.

Here are the three basic operations of gematria:

Addition: This involves adding the numerical values of the letters in a word or phrase to get a final numerical value.

For example, the word "chai" (חי) has a numerical value of 18 (8+10).

Subtraction involves subtracting the numerical values of one word or phrase from another to determine their difference. For example, the difference between the numerical values of the phrase "*Mashiach*" (משיח), meaning "*Messiah*," and "*satan*" (שטן), meaning "*adversary*," is 359 (358-1).

Equivalence: This involves finding words or phrases with the same numerical value. Words or phrases with the same numerical value are believed to be connected in some way and may reveal hidden meanings or relationships.

For example, the words "*sin*" (חטא) and "*purification*" (טהרה) both have a numerical value of 18.

These operations can be applied to individual words, entire phrases, or even multiple words and phrases together.

The resulting numerical values, according to gematria practitioners, can reveal hidden connections and insights into the spiritual and mystical significance of the words and phrases involved.

Methods of Calculation

———

G ematria employs a variety of computation methods, each with its own set of rules and variants.

Here are some of the most common methods:

Standard Gematria: This is the most basic method of gematria, in which each Hebrew letter is assigned a fixed numerical value, as described earlier. The numerical value of a word is calculated by adding up the values of its letters.

Reduced Gematria: This method involves reducing the numerical value of a word or phrase to a single digit by repeatedly adding up its numbers. For example, the word "chai" (חי) has a numerical value of 18, which is reduced to 9 (1+8). This method often finds connections between words and phrases with the same single-digit value.

Integral reduced Gematria: This is a variation of reduced gematria that involves reducing the numerical value of a word or phrase to a single digit using a different formula.

The value of each letter is reduced to a single number using this method by dividing it by nine and taking the remainder.

For example, the letter "*chet*" (ח) has a value of 8, which is reduced to 8 (8 divided by 9 has a remainder of 8). The final numerical value is obtained by adding the letters' decreasing importance and reducing the sum to a single digit.

Reverse Gematria: This method involves assigning numerical values to the letters of the alphabet in reverse order so that the letter "aleph" (א) has a value of 22, the letter "bet" (ב) has a value of 21, and so on.

A word's numerical value is then determined by summing the importance of its letters in reverse order. This strategy is occasionally used to discover links between words and sentences that are opposite or complementary in some way.

These are just a few examples of the different calculation methods used in gematria.

Other approaches include ordinal gematria, which assigns numerical values based on alphabetical order, and atbash, which replaces each letter with its counterpart at the opposite end of the alphabet.

Examples of Gematria in the Hebrew Bible

G ematria is a means of deciphering and revealing hidden meanings in the Hebrew Bible, and there are several examples of gematria in biblical writings.

Here are some examples:

The word for "*light*" (אור) has a numerical value of 207.

The word for "*secret*" (סוד) also has a numerical value of 207.

This connection suggests that the secrets of God are revealed through the light of His wisdom.

The word for "*truth*" (אמת) has a numerical value of 1+40+400=441.

The word for "*peace*" (שלום) also has a numerical value of 1+30+40+6=77.

According to gematria, these two words are connected because their numerical values are both perfect squares (*21 squared and 11 squared, respectively*).

This suggests that peace is the result of living in truth.

The name of God, YHWH (יהוה), has a numerical value of 26. This is also the numerical value of the Hebrew word for "*name*" (שם).

This connection suggests that the name of God is holy and powerful and represents His essence and attributes.

The number 7 is considered a sacred number in the Hebrew Bible and is often used in gematria to represent completion or perfection.

For example, the seventh day of creation is the day of rest, and the menorah in the temple has seven branches.

The word for "*seven*" (שבע) has a numerical value of 372, which is equal to the numerical value of the Hebrew word for "*oath*" (שבועה).

This connection suggests that an oath is a binding commitment that completes or perfects a promise or agreement.

These are just a few examples of Gematria in the Hebrew Bible, which is said to reveal hidden connections and meanings in the text.

III. Gematria in Jewish Mysticism

———

Gematria is an important tool in Jewish mysticism, particularly in Kabbalah, Judaism's spiritual tradition. Kabbalists believe that the numerical values of Hebrew words and letters have heavenly significance and can be used to reveal deeper spiritual truths in the text.

The Zohar, a mystical commentary on the Torah, is one of the most well-known Kabbalistic texts that heavily uses gematria.

The numerical values of words and letters are used in the Zohar to disclose the hidden meanings of biblical stories and to expose the mystical secrets of the universe.

Kabbalists also use gematria to study the names of God, which are considered sacred and powerful.

By understanding the numerical values of the various names of God, Kabbalists believe they can tap into the divine energy and draw closer to God.

In addition to normal Gematria, Kabbalists use notarikon, which includes constructing new words by combining the first letters of many words, and Temurah, which involves rearranging the letters of a word or phrase to produce a new meaning.

Gematria is crucial in Jewish mysticism because it is said to provide a method of deciphering the hidden meanings and divine mysteries inherent in the Hebrew language and the Hebrew Bible.

Kabbalistic Interpretation of Gematria

―――――

G ematria is viewed as a means of gaining greater degrees of understanding and insight into the divine mysteries of the universe in Kabbalistic interpretation.

Every word, letter, and number has a spiritual meaning and is linked to the divine energies that flow through the universe, according to Kabbalah.

According to Kabbalists, the numerical values of words and letters are not arbitrary but rather part of a wider system of divine correspondences that connect the physical and spiritual worlds.

Kabbalists believe that through comprehending the numerical values of words and letters, they can acquire insights into the secret meanings of the Torah, God's names, and the spiritual forces that control the universe.

One of the fundamental concepts of Kabbalistic interpretation is that words and letters are continually evolving and changing entities.

Kabbalists believe that changing the numerical values of words and letters allows them to access the spiritual forces and divine mysteries contained within them.

Kabbalists, for example, may employ gematria to discover hidden connections between seemingly unrelated words or phrases or to discover the mystical significance of specific numbers or numerical patterns.

They might also use gematria to create new words or phrases that capture deeper levels of meaning or reveal hidden connections between different aspects of the divine.

Overall, the Kabbalistic interpretation of gematria is a method of accessing the spiritual dimensions of the Hebrew language and the universe and discovering divine mysteries concealed beneath the surface of everyday life.

Use Of Gematria In Jewish Magic

Gematria has also been used in Jewish magic, specifically in the creation of amulets and talismans.

Amulets are artefacts said to have protective properties. Conversely, Talismans are artefacts believed to have unique powers or talents, such as the ability to heal, attract love, or bring commercial success.

In Jewish magic, amulets and talismans are often inscribed with words or phrases with particular numerical values based on gematria.

The belief is that by creating a physical object that embodies the numerical values of certain words or phrases, the object becomes charged with spiritual energy and can be used to influence the course of events in the physical world.

For example, an amulet might be inscribed with the numerical value of the Hebrew word for "*protection*," or the name of a powerful angel or spirit, to protect evil forces.

To bring success in a certain endeavour, a talisman could be imprinted with the numerical value of a specific verse from the Torah.

In some cases, Jewish magic also uses gematria to create secret names or codes believed to have powerful spiritual significance.

These names or codes could be employed in spells or ceremonies to summon spiritual entities or achieve specific purposes.

The use of Gematria in Jewish magic shows a belief in the power of words and numbers to influence physical events, as well as the importance of channelling spiritual energies to achieve one's objectives.

Role Of Gematria In Jewish Esoteric Traditions

━━━

G ematria is used extensively in Jewish esoteric traditions such as Kabbalah, Hasidic mysticism, and Jewish magic.

In these traditions, gematria is regarded as a means of discovering the hidden meanings and mystical aspects of the Hebrew language and the universe.

One of the key aspects of Gematria in Jewish esoteric traditions is the belief that every letter and word in the Hebrew language has a divine origin and spiritual significance.

According to this belief, the Hebrew language is not just a communication system but a sacred vehicle for conveying divine wisdom and energy.

In Kabbalah, Gematria is used to uncover the deeper meanings of the Torah and other sacred texts and gain insights into God's nature and the universe.

Kabbalists use gematria to explore the relationships between different words and phrases and to identify hidden connections and correspondences between seemingly unrelated concepts.

In Hasidic mysticism, gematria is used as a tool for spiritual transformation and self-improvement.

According to Hasidic teachers, concentrating on the numerical values of words and letters helps purify and refine one's inner self, allowing one to achieve higher degrees of spiritual awareness and connection to God.

Gematria is used in Jewish magic to produce amulets and talismans as well as to summon spiritual forces and energies.

Jewish magicians utilise gematria to generate coded names and formulas that are said to have powerful spiritual power and can be used to influence the forces of the universe to achieve their purposes.

Gematria is regarded as a potent instrument for accessing the universe's hidden realms and uncovering the secrets of heavenly wisdom and power in Jewish esoteric traditions.

Examples Of Gematria In Jewish Mystical Texts

In Jewish mystical books such as the Zohar, the Sefer Yetzirah, and the writings of the Arizal (*Rabbi Isaac Luria*), gematria is often utilised to investigate the hidden meanings of Hebrew words and to reveal profound insights into the nature of God and the cosmos.

Here are some examples of Gematria in Jewish mystical texts:

The Zohar: In the Zohar, a central text of Kabbalah, the numerical value of the Hebrew word "*yachad*" (*together*) is 18, and the numerical value of the Hebrew word "*echad*" (*one*) is also 18.

This connection teaches that individuals can experience a higher spiritual oneness with God when they unite.

The Sefer Yetzirah: The Sefer Yetzirah, an early Kabbalistic text, assigns each Hebrew letter to one of the four elements (*fire, air, water, and earth*) and one of the planets in the solar system.

The numerical value of each letter is also associated with specific meanings and correspondences.

The writings of the Arizal: Rabbi Isaac Luria, also known as the Arizal, was a 16th-century Kabbalist who developed a Kabbalistic meditation and prayer system.

In his works, he used gematria to investigate the mystical meanings of Hebrew words and to uncover hidden links between various parts of the Torah.

For example, he notes that the numerical value of the word "tzitzit" (*the fringes worn on the corners of a prayer shawl*) is 600, corresponding to the six hundred thousand souls said to have been present at the giving of the Torah at Mount Sinai.

The Baal Shem Tov: Rabbi Israel ben Eliezer, also known as the Baal Shem Tov, founded the Hasidic movement in the 18th century.

He used gematria in his teachings to investigate the mystical aspects of the Torah and to educate his students on how to connect with God through prayer and meditation.

For example, he noted that the numerical value of the Hebrew word "*yirah*" (fear) is the same as the numerical value of the Hebrew word "*ahavah*" (love), teaching that true fear of God is rooted in love and devotion.

IV. Gematria in Christianity

———

While most people identify Gematria with Jewish mysticism and Kabbalah, it has also been used in Christian traditions, particularly early Christianity and biblical numerology.

Here are some examples of Gematria in Christianity:

Early Christian writers, such as Irenaeus and Clement of Alexandria, employed gematria to investigate the symbolic implications of numbers in the Bible.

For example, they noted that the number 888 (*the numerical value of the Greek letters in the name Jesus*) was associated with the resurrection since Jesus rose from the dead on the eighth day.

Biblical numerology: Gematria is also used in the study of biblical numerology, which explores the symbolic significance of numbers in the Bible.

For example, seven is often associated with completion or perfection since God rested on the seventh day after creating the world, and there are seven days a week.

The number 40 is often associated with purification or testing since Moses and Elijah both fasted for 40 days, and Jesus spent 40 days in the wilderness.

Christian mysticism: Gematria was employed for spiritual thought and contemplation by some Christian mystics, including St. John of the Cross and St. Teresa of Avila.

They would meditate on the numerical values of words or phrases in the Bible, seeking to uncover hidden meanings and insights into the nature of God and the soul.

Modern Christian writers: Some contemporary Christian writers, such as John Michell and Richard Heath, have used gematria in their studies of sacred geometry and geometric patterns in the Bible and Christian architecture.

They regard gematria as a tool for studying the relationship between the physical and spiritual realms and unlocking the hidden significance and symbolism of these patterns.

The Book of Revelation: Gematria is also used in the Book of Revelation, the Christian Bible's final book, which is replete with symbolic numbers and enigmatic messages. For example, 666 is associated with the book's "*beast*" or "*Antichrist*" and has been the topic of considerable discussion and interpretation throughout history.

Popular Christian numerology: Gematria and Christian numerology have been popularised in modern culture through books, movies, and music.

Dan Brown's best-selling novel "*The Da Vinci Code*," mostly fiction, for example, analyses the usage of gematria and other numerical codes in Christian history.

On the other hand, bands such as Tool and Slayer have employed numerology and gematria in their music and album artwork.

While gematria has a long and rich history in Jewish mysticism, it has also impacted Christian thought and spirituality, particularly in the study of biblical numerology and esoteric traditions.

Whether used as a tool for meditation and contemplation or to explore the hidden meanings and symbolism in sacred texts, gematria remains a fascinating and enigmatic subject for scholars and seekers alike.

It is important to note that Christian views on gematria vary widely, and opinions on its appropriateness or usefulness may depend on individual beliefs and interpretations.

Some Christians may regard gematria as a useful tool for delving into the symbolic meaning of numbers in the Bible and Christian heritage.

Others, on the other hand, may see it as a potentially hazardous or deceptive practice that detracts from the genuine meaning and message of Scripture.

Finally, the interpretation and use of gematria is a question of personal faith and conscience, and each person must determine what is appropriate and beneficial to their spiritual journey.

Christian Use Of Gematria In The Early Church

G ematria appears to have been utilised sparingly in the early Christian Church.

While certain early Christian writers, such as Saint Augustine, recognised the symbolic value of numbers in the Bible and utilised numerology in their exegesis of Scripture, no proof exists that they expressly used gematria.

Many early Christian writers were cautious about using any mystical or esoteric practices in their interpretation of Scripture, as they believed that the true meaning of the Bible was accessible through *the guidance of the Holy Spirit* and sounded exegetical methods.

However, when Christianity grew and encountered various cultures and traditions, it is probable that Jewish and Hellenistic numerological traditions that used gematria affected certain Christian thinkers.

Some early Christian Gnostic manuscripts, for example, the Gospel of Thomas, contain numerical puzzles and codes that may be related to gematria.

While gematria does not appear to have been a common practice in the early Christian Church, the use of numerology and symbolic numbers in Christian theology and exegesis has a long and rich history that continues to the present day.

Christian scholars did not become more widely known or employ gematria until the Middle Ages.

However, many Christian intellectuals became interested in Kabbalah and Jewish mystical traditions during this period, which included gematria as an important technique for reading Scripture and revealing hidden meanings.

One notable example is the 13th-century Spanish mystic and theologian Ramon Llull, who developed a system of mystical theology based on the principles of gematria and other numerological practices.

Llull believed that hidden, symbolic meanings existed in all aspects of creation, including words and letters, and that these meanings could be disclosed using numbers and mathematical principles.

Similarly, the 16th-century German theologian Johannes Reuchlin was a prominent advocate of Kabbalistic study, including gematria.

Reuchlin contended that Kabbalistic teachings and gematria might help people better understand Christian theology and Scripture.

And that the symbolic meanings revealed by numerology might assist Christians in drawing closer to God.

Despite these early examples, gematria did not become widespread in Christian theology and exegesis until much later.

It remained a somewhat marginal area of study within the Christian tradition.

Nonetheless, it remains a source of fascination for some academics and spiritual searchers who feel that using mathematics and symbolism might bring new insights and revelations into the secrets of the Christian faith.

Gematria In Christian Mysticism And Symbolism

Gematria is frequently utilised in Christian mysticism and symbolism to understand Scripture and reveal hidden truths in the Bible.

Some Christian mystics believe that every creation component, including numbers and letters, holds a spiritual value that can be revealed through gematria.

One example of the use of Gematria in Christian mysticism is found in the works of the 16th-century German mystic and theologian Jakob Böhme.

Böhme believed that the numbers and letters of the Hebrew and Greek alphabets contained profound spiritual truths and that the principles of gematria could be used to uncover these truths.

He used gematria extensively in his mystical writings, and many of his followers believed that his insights into the spiritual significance of numbers and letters were divinely inspired.

Similarly, Carl Jung, a 20th-century Swiss psychologist and Christian mystic, believed that Gematria principles might be utilised to unearth hidden meaning in the Bible and other spiritual works.

Jung felt that the Hebrew and Greek alphabets contained archetypal symbols that might be utilised to decipher the deeper meanings of Scripture and gain insight into the human mind.

Other Christian mystics have used gematria as a tool for meditation and contemplation, believing that the repetition of numerical sequences and symbolic patterns can help them to enter into deeper states of spiritual awareness and connection with God.

While gematria is a fairly peripheral field of study within the Christian faith, it remains a source of wonder and interest for many spiritual searchers and scholars.

Use Of Gematria In Christian Apologetics

———

Some Christian apologists have also employed gematria to argue the Bible's authenticity and authority.

Christian apologists who use gematria often argue that the numerical patterns and symbolic meanings found in Scripture provide evidence for the divine inspiration and accuracy of the Bible.

One example of the use of Gematria in Christian apologetics is found in the works of the 17th-century English theologian and mathematician John Lightfoot.

Lightfoot used gematria to argue that the biblical text had been preserved in its original form and that the numerical patterns and symbolic meanings found in Scripture could not have been produced by human authors alone.

Similarly, the 20th-century American evangelist Ivan Panin used gematria to argue for the divine inspiration of the Bible.

Panin believed that the numerical patterns found in the Bible, including patterns of word frequencies and verse counts, provided mathematical evidence for the accuracy and authority of the biblical text.

While the use of Gematria in Christian apologetics is still debated, some apologists continue to employ numerical patterns and symbolic meanings as proof of the Bible's supernatural inspiration and truth.

However, other Christian scholars and theologians argue that the use of gematria to defend the Bible's authority is incorrect because the genuine basis of the Bible's authority resides in its spiritual teachings and moral counsel.

NB. Apologetics is a discipline of theology that seeks to defend and justify the fundamentals of a certain religious religion, frequently in the face of criticism, scepticism, or hostility from those who do not share that faith.

It entails offering reasoned arguments and evidence to support a religious tradition's beliefs and practices, as well as responding to criticisms or challenges brought against them. The word "apologetics" is derived from the Greek word "apologia," which signifies a defence or justification.

Examples Of Gematria In The New Testament

———

The use of gematria in the New Testament is less common than in the Old Testament and Jewish mysticism.

Some academics, however, have discovered multiple instances of gematria in the New Testament, particularly in the Book of Revelation.

One of the most famous examples of Gematria in the New Testament is the number of the Beast, mentioned in **Revelation 13:18**.

In this passage, the Beast is described as having a number, which is said to be *666*.

Some scholars have suggested that this number represents a numerical code, with each of the three digits representing a specific letter in the Greek alphabet.

Scholars have given many interpretations of what the number might indicate by applying gematria to this code, such as the name of a specific historical individual or a symbolic representation of evil.

Another example of Gematria in the New Testament is the story of the miraculous fish catch in **John 21:11**. In this passage, Jesus instructs his disciples to cast their net on the right side of the boat, and they *catch 153 fish*.

Some experts believe this number is a coded message, with each digit representing a different letter of the Greek alphabet.

By applying gematria to this code, scholars have proposed various interpretations of what the number might symbolise, including a representation of the unity of the Church or a symbolic representation of the total number of people who will be saved.

While gematria is not as prevalent in the New Testament as it is in the Old Testament and Jewish mysticism, some scholars feel that the employment of numerical codes and symbolic meanings throughout the Bible demonstrates the biblical text's complexity and multi-layered character.

V. Gematria In Other Cultures

———

The concept of giving numerical values to letters and words, known as gematria, is not unique to Hebrew or Jewish culture.

Similar practices exist in other cultures and languages worldwide, including *Greek, Arabic, and Chinese.*

In ancient Greece, the practice of isopsephy involved assigning numerical values to letters in the Greek alphabet.

This practice was used in various forms of Greek mysticism and philosophy, including Pythagoreanism and the study of the Kabbalah in the Hellenistic era.

In Arabic culture, abjad numerals involve assigning numerical values to letters in the Arabic alphabet.

This practice is used in various Islamic mysticism and divination forms, including interpreting dreams and using talismans and amulets.

Chinese numerology involves assigning numerical values to the strokes used to write Chinese characters in Chinese culture.

This approach is employed in numerous traditional Chinese medicine and divination forms, such as feng shui and I Ching interpretation.

While the specific methods and practises of gematria differ throughout cultures and languages, the core premise of assigning numerical values to letters and words to unearth hidden meanings and symbolic patterns remains consistent.

Gematria In Greek And Latin Alphabets

———

The technique of giving numerical values to letters and words, known as gematria, is not unique to the Hebrew script. It appears in the Greek and Latin alphabets as well.

Isopsephy was a process in ancient Greece that entailed assigning numerical values to letters in the Greek alphabet.

The system was based on the principle that the letters of the alphabet represented specific numerical values, with the first nine letters representing the numbers one through nine.

The practice of isopsephy was used in various forms of Greek mysticism and philosophy, including Pythagoreanism, which explored the mystical relationship between numbers and the universe.

In Latin, the practice of gematria was known as "*numerology*" and involved assigning numerical values to letters in the alphabet.

The practice was utilised in mediaeval Christianity to investigate the mystical implications of biblical passages and in mediaeval Jewish mysticism to investigate the hidden meanings of Hebrew words.

While the specific methods and practises of gematria differ throughout cultures and languages, the core premise of assigning numerical values to letters and words to reveal hidden meanings and symbolic patterns stays consistent.

Gematria In Islamic Numerology

———

G ematria is known as "*Abjad numerals*" in Islamic culture. This is because it entails assigning numerical values to letters in the Arabic script.

The system is based on the principle that each Arabic alphabet represents a specific numerical value, with the first ten letters representing the numbers one through ten.

Abjad numerals are used in various forms of Islamic mysticism and divination, including interpreting dreams and using talismans and amulets.

Islamic scholars and mystics believe that the letters of the Arabic alphabet have inherent mystical qualities and that the numerical values assigned to them can reveal hidden meanings and symbolic patterns in the Qur'an and other sacred texts.

In addition to its use in Islamic mysticism, Abjad numerals are also used in mundane everyday life, such as for numbering items or assigning numerical values to dates.

While the specific methods and practises of gematria differ between cultures and religions, the core premise of assigning numerical values to letters and words to unearth hidden meanings and symbolic patterns remains consistent.

Gematria in Hinduism

———

Gematria is not as widely used in Hinduism as Judaism, Christianity, and Islam.

However, Hinduism has a long tradition of assigning numerical values to letters and words for various purposes, including sacred text interpretation and numerology.

In Hinduism, assigning numerical values to letters and words is known as "*yantra*" or "*mandala*". Likewise, these geometric symbols used in meditation and contemplation incorporate letters and numbers.

They are believed to represent the cosmos and the divine principles of the universe.

The numerical values assigned to letters and words in yantra and mandala are based on the ancient Sanskrit language.

Each letter of the Sanskrit alphabet has a numerical value, and these values are used to create complex geometric patterns that are believed to have a spiritual and mystical significance.

In addition to using yantra and mandala, Hinduism also has a tradition of using numerology for divination and fortune-telling.

This entails assigning numerical numbers to names and birthdates to uncover hidden qualities and potential future events.

While gematria is not a major practice in Hinduism, it is an important aspect of Hindu spiritual traditions to use numerical values in various sorts of sacred and mystical acts.

Gematria in Chinese numerology

———

There is a long tradition in Chinese numerology of giving numerical values to words and names based on their pronunciation sounds in the Chinese language. This method is known as *"pi-gua"* or *"ba-gua,"* which translates as *"eight trigrams."*

The pi-gua system assigns a numerical value to each of the eight trigrams, representing the elements of the natural world and various aspects of human experience.

These numerical values can then be used to analyse and interpret the meanings of names and words and predict the outcome of future events.

In addition to the pi-gua system, Chinese numerology also uses the *"five elements"* system, which assigns numerical values to the five elements of wood, fire, earth, metal, and water.

These elements are believed to represent different aspects of the natural world and various parts of human experience and personality.

Chinese numerology is also used in various forms of divination and fortune-telling, such as the I Ching or *"Book of Changes,"* which uses hexagrams composed of six lines to represent different combinations of yin and yang, the two fundamental principles of the universe.

While gematria, as it is traditionally understood in Jewish, Christian, and Islamic mysticism, is not a central practice in Chinese numerology.

Nevertheless, assigning numerical values to words and names for divinatory and interpretive purposes is an important aspect of Chinese spiritual traditions.

Chinese numerology also uses the concept of "*lucky numbers*" and "*unlucky numbers*," which are believed to influence various aspects of life, such as love, career, and health.

For example, the number 8 is considered a lucky number because it sounds close to the phrase for "*prosperity*" in Chinese. The number four, on the other hand, is considered unlucky since it sounds similar to the word "*death*."

The concept of assigning numerical values to words and names is also utilised in the Chinese zodiac, which gives one of 12 animal signs to each year based on Jupiter's 12-year round around the sun.

Each animal sign is associated with certain personality traits, lucky numbers, and auspicious days for various activities.

Overall, many spiritual and mystical traditions around the world, including those of China, India, and the Middle East, assign numerical values to words and names for divinatory and interpretative purposes.

While the precise methods and beliefs differ, the underlying premise that language and numerology are interconnected and can reveal deeper truths about the universe and human experience is powerful and enduring.

VI. Criticisms and Controversies

———

Gematria has been the subject of criticism and controversy throughout history, particularly from sceptics questioning the practice's legitimacy and its mystical and divinatory features.

The following are some of the most common arguments and issues about gematria:

Lack of empirical evidence: Many sceptics contend that no scientific or empirical proof giving numerical values to words and names may disclose hidden meanings or predict future events.

They see gematria as a purely subjective and speculative practice lacking any objective reality basis.

Selective interpretation: Critics also argue that gematria relies on the particular interpretation of texts and symbols and can be used to support almost any interpretation, depending on the practitioner's biases and assumptions.

This can lead to misunderstanding and dispute since different practitioners may assign different numerical values to the same texts or symbols and reach different conclusions.

Occult associations: Gematria has often been associated with occult and mystical practices, which has led to suspicion and criticism from some religious and cultural groups.

Some practitioners of gematria have been accused of engaging in demonic or forbidden activities, which has further fueled controversy and mistrust.

Cultural appropriation: In recent years, some scholars and activists have raised concerns about the cultural appropriation of gematria and other mystical practices from non-Western cultures.

They argue that Western practitioners may be appropriating and misusing these practices without fully understanding their cultural and historical contexts, which can lead to misunderstandings and misrepresentations.

Despite these criticisms and debates, many people worldwide use and study gematria as a beneficial tool for delving into the deeper meanings and secrets of language and numerology.

While the legitimacy and accuracy of gematria are debatable, its continuing appeal and intrigue imply that it will remain a source of fascination and research for many years.

Sceptical Views Of Gematria

―――

Sceptics of Gematria raise various concerns, including the following:

Lack of scientific evidence: Many sceptics argue that gematria lacks any scientific basis and that no empirical evidence supports the idea that assigning numerical values to words and phrases can reveal hidden meanings or predict future events.

Selective interpretation: Skeptics also point out that gematria relies on the selective interpretation of texts and symbols and can be used to support almost any interpretation, depending on the practitioner's biases and assumptions.

This can lead to confusion and disagreement, as different practitioners may assign different numerical values and arrive at different conclusions based on the same texts or symbols.

Confirmation bias: Sceptics argue that gematria can be subject to confirmation bias. Practitioners look for evidence to support their pre-existing beliefs and assumptions while ignoring or dismissing evidence that contradicts them.

This can result in a distorted perspective of reality and the reinforcement of false ideas and superstitions.

Pseudoscience: Some sceptics view gematria as a form of pseudoscience in which practitioners claim to use scientific or mathematical methods to uncover hidden meanings or patterns in language but rely on subjective and unproven assumptions.

Despite these criticisms, many individuals continue to practise and study gematria, seeing it as a beneficial tool for delving into the deeper meanings and secrets of language and numerology.

While the legitimacy and accuracy of gematria are debatable, its continuing appeal and intrigue imply that it will remain a source of fascination and research for many years.

Criticisms From Within The Jewish Tradition

―――――

While gematria has been a part of Jewish history for generations, there are some objections and disagreements among Jews.

Some of the common criticisms include the following:

Misinterpretation: Gematria can be easily misinterpreted or manipulated to arrive at conclusions that may not be consistent with the original intent or meaning of the text. This can lead to confusion or even misrepresentation of the original text.

Idolatry: Some Jewish scholars argue that gematria can be used as a form of idolatry by placing too much emphasis on the numerical value of words and phrases rather than their spiritual or ethical significance.

Overemphasis: Some Jewish communities may emphasise gematria excessively, to the point where it becomes the primary focus of their studies or religious practice.

This can lead to a neglect of other important aspects of Jewish tradition and spirituality.

Lack of authority: Gematria is not considered authoritative in Jewish tradition and is often viewed as a form of interpretation rather than a definitive source of truth.

Some scholars argue that this lack of authority can make distinguishing legitimate insights from arbitrary or fanciful interpretations difficult.

Despite these criticisms, gematria remains an important aspect of Jewish tradition and is widely practised and studied by many Jewish scholars and communities.

As with any interpretation or spiritual practice, it is vital to approach gematria with a critical and discerning mind rather than as a substitute for spiritual growth or ethical conduct.

Theological Debates Over The Use Of Gematria In Christianity

The usage of Gematria in Christianity has long been a source of theological dispute.

According to certain Christian scholars, gematria is a useful tool for deciphering the deeper meaning of biblical passages and revealing hidden patterns and relationships.

Others, however, are sceptical of its integrity and caution against reading too much into number patterns or making unsubstantiated statements based on gematria.

One of the main debates surrounding the use of Gematria in Christianity is whether it is appropriate to use non-biblical sources, such as Greek or Hebrew mythology, to interpret numerical patterns in the Bible.

Some scholars worry that this could lead to syncretism and fuzziness in the lines between Christian and pagan practices.

Others, on the other hand, believe there is merit in connecting different religious traditions and investigating the common themes and symbols that underpin them.

Another issue of debate is whether gematria should be utilised to make particular future predictions or prophesies, such as predicting the end times or identifying the Antichrist.

According to some scholars, this can lead to a type of biblical numerology closer to divination than biblical interpretation.

Others, on the other hand, think that gematria has a genuine role in comprehending the prophetic nature of Scripture.

Overall, the usage of Gematria in Christianity is still a contentious issue that sparks theological disputes and discussions among researchers and practitioners.

While gematria can provide useful insights and connections, it is vital to approach it with caution and discernment to avoid making unsupported assertions or drawing unjustified conclusions based solely on numerical patterns.

Contemporary Controversies Surrounding Gematria

In contemporary times, gematria has continued to be a source of controversy and debate.

One area of controversy is the use of gematria in modern-day numerology and divination practices.

Some practitioners of these arts claim to use gematria as a tool for predicting the future or understanding personal characteristics based on a person's name or birth date.

However, this use of gematria has been criticised by many as being unscientific and lacking in any real predictive power.

Another area of controversy is the use of gematria in conspiracy theories and fringe interpretations of historical events.

Some proponents of these theories claim to have uncovered hidden messages and patterns in historical events based on gematria, leading to claims of secret societies, encoded messages, and hidden agendas.

However, these claims have been widely criticised by mainstream scholars and historians as lacking any real evidence or historical validity.

Finally, some critics argue that using gematria in any context is inherently flawed. It relies on arbitrary numerical associations and can be used to "*prove*" almost any point, depending on how the numbers are interpreted.

They argue that gematria is a form of *numerological speculation* with no real basis in the original meaning of biblical or other religious texts and should not be given any more weight than other forms of numerology or divination.

VII. Applications of Gematria

———

Gematria has numerous uses in a variety of fields, including:

Biblical and religious studies: Gematria is used to analyse and interpret the numerical values of words and phrases in religious texts, including the Hebrew Bible, the New Testament, and the Quran.

Jewish mysticism: Gematria plays a central role in Jewish mystical traditions, such as Kabbalah, where it is used to uncover hidden meanings and connections between different aspects of the divine.

Christian mysticism and symbolism: Gematria is also used in Christian mysticism and symbolism to interpret the hidden meanings and connections between biblical texts and other spiritual teachings.

Numerology and divination: Gematria is used by certain numerologists and psychics to decipher a person's personality traits from their name and date of birth.

Cryptography and coding: Gematria has been used in cryptography and coding to encode and decode messages and create hidden messages and patterns in text. Similar to the forthcoming digital currency, cryptocurrency? I wonder!

Linguistics and language analysis: Gematria has been used in linguistic and language analysis to study the relationships between different languages and to uncover hidden patterns and meanings in language.

Mathematics and science: Gematria has also been utilised in mathematics and science to investigate number relationships and discover hidden patterns and connections in numerical data.

Use Of Gematria In Biblical Exegesis

A s previously noted, gematria has been utilised in biblical exegesis to unearth hidden meanings and connections between various parts of the Bible.

The use of gematria in biblical exegesis can be traced back to early Jewish and Christian traditions when it was believed that the numerical values of words and phrases contained significant symbolic and mystical importance.

Gematria was employed in Jewish tradition to interpret the Hebrew Bible, notably the Torah.

Rabbis and scholars used gematria to uncover hidden meanings and connections between different parts of the Torah and to explore the relationships between various aspects of Jewish theology and mysticism.

Gematria was also used to understand the relationships between different Hebrew words and reveal the Hebrew language's deeper meanings.

In Christian tradition, gematria was also used in biblical exegesis, particularly in interpreting the New Testament.

Early Christian theologians believed that the numerical values of words and phrases held important symbolic and mystical significance.

Therefore, they used gematria to uncover hidden meanings and connections between different parts of the New Testament.

Gematria was also used to understand the relationships between different aspects of the link between Christ and the Holy Spirit is an example of Christian theology and mysticism.

Gematria is still employed in biblical exegesis, particularly in Jewish and Christian studies.

While some scholars regard gematria as a useful tool for revealing hidden meanings and connections in religious texts, others view it as an untrustworthy and subjective approach to interpretation.

Gematria In Contemporary Spiritual Practices

———

In biblical interpretation, gematria has been utilised to find hidden meanings and connections between different passages of the Bible.

The use of gematria in biblical exegesis can be traced back to early Jewish and Christian traditions when it was believed that the numerical values of words and phrases contained significant symbolic and mystical importance.

In Jewish tradition, gematria was used to interpret the Hebrew Bible, particularly the Torah.

Rabbis and scholars used gematria to uncover hidden meanings and connections between different parts of the Torah and to explore the relationships between various aspects of Jewish theology and mysticism.

Gematria was also used to understand the relationships between different Hebrew words and reveal the Hebrew language's deeper meanings.

In Christian tradition, gematria was also used in biblical exegesis, particularly in interpreting the New Testament.

Early Christian theologians believed that the numerical values of words and phrases held important symbolic and mystical significance.

Therefore, they used gematria to uncover hidden meanings and connections between different parts of the New Testament.

Gematria was also used to understand the relationships between different aspects of Christian theology and mysticism, such as the relationship between Christ and the Holy Spirit.

Gematria continues to be used in biblical exegesis, particularly in Jewish and Christian scholarship.

While some scholars view gematria as a valuable tool for uncovering hidden meanings and connections in religious texts, others criticise it as an unreliable and subjective method of interpretation.

Contemporary Spiritual Practices

In addition to its historical use in Jewish and Christian traditions, gematria has also been incorporated into contemporary spiritual practices in various ways.

In some New Age and occult practices, gematria is used as a tool for divination and predicting future events.

Words and phrases are assigned numerical values and then used to produce predictions.

However, this application of gematria is controversial and has been criticised as untrustworthy and lacking scientific data.

Gematria is also used in modern spiritual pursuits such as meditation and contemplation.

Practitioners aim to unearth hidden meanings and connections between different areas of their spiritual practice by focusing on the numerical values of words and phrases.

Gematria has also been utilised by several contemporary scholars in their study of comparative religion and mystical traditions.

Scholars attempt to discover commonalities and links between diverse mystical traditions by investigating the usage of gematria in various religious and cultural contexts.

Overall, gematria in contemporary spiritual practices is still a source of contention.

While some regard it as a beneficial instrument for spiritual inquiry and progress, others view it as a subjective and untrustworthy way of interpretation.

Gematria In Numerology And Divination

G ematria has been used in various forms of numerology and divination.

In numerology, the numerical values assigned to letters and words are believed to hold esoteric or mystical significance.

These values create charts and calculations that offer insight into a person's personality traits, life path, and future.

Gematria has also been incorporated into various forms of divination, such as tarot card readings and astrology.

In these practices, gematria is used to interpret the meanings of symbols and numbers in a way that provides insight into a person's life, relationships, and future.

However, the use of gematria in numerology and divination is controversial and has been criticised by sceptics and traditionalists who view it as a superstitious or unscientific practice.

Some scholars argue that there is no empirical evidence to support the claims made by proponents of gematria-based numerology and divination and that these practices are based on subjective interpretations rather than objective facts.

Despite these criticisms, gematria in numerology and divination remains popular among many practitioners who view it as a valuable tool for spiritual exploration and self-discovery.

Gematria In Modern-Day Cryptography And Code-Breaking

―――

Gematria is also used in current cryptography and code-breaking.

Using numerical values assigned to letters and words can assist in creating intricate codes that are difficult to interpret without understanding the gematria system.

Gematria-based codes have been utilised in various applications, including military communications, banking, and internet security.

To prevent unauthorised access, gematria-based codes have been employed in some circumstances to encrypt sensitive information such as passwords and credit card data.

On the other hand, the use of gematria in cryptography is contentious. Some experts believe it makes codes more vulnerable to attacks by skilled hackers who are conversant with gematria-based encryption schemes.

Despite these reservations, researchers and practitioners in information security continue to investigate and enhance the application of gematria in current cryptography and code-breaking.

VIII. Conclusion

———

Finally, gematria is an intriguing and sophisticated technique for giving numerical values to letters and words in many languages.

For ages, scholars, mystics, and practitioners from various countries and traditions have researched and disputed its history, use, and application.

Gematria has been used in biblical exegesis, Jewish mysticism, Christian symbolism and apologetics, and diverse spiritual activities.

It is also used in cryptography and code-breaking, which can be advantageous and problematic.

While gematria has its detractors and debates, its ongoing attraction and relevancy indicate that it will, as previously stated, be researched and argued for many years to come.

Summary Of Key Points

———

Here are a few highlights: gematria:
Gematria is a way of assigning numerical values to letters or words with a long history in Jewish, Christian, and other cultural traditions.

Gematria can be utilised for various reasons, including the interpretation of religious texts, the exploration of mystical concepts, and even cryptography and code-breaking.

Gematria has long been a source of contention, with sceptics and critics disputing its veracity and religious leaders warning against its misuse or over-reliance.

Regardless of these arguments, gematria remains a powerful instrument for investigating the links between language, symbolism, and spirituality, and it continues to inspire people from various traditions and practises.

This book introduced gematria by delving into its history, methodology, and applications in many civilisations and religious situations.

It also discusses some objections and debates surrounding gematria and urges readers to incorporate this interesting and frequently mysterious technique into their spiritual journeys.

Reflection On The Significance Of Gematria

Gematria is an enthralling and intricate system of assigning numerical values to letters and words in several languages, notably Hebrew.

Its roots can be traced back to ancient societies, and it has been applied in various domains, including theology, mysticism, and divination.

Gematria has been employed extensively in Jewish and Christian traditions to convey deeper interpretations and insights into sacred writings.

In Jewish mysticism, numerical values of words and phrases are thought to reveal hidden meanings and connections between seemingly unconnected concepts.

In Christian apologetics, gematria has been used to demonstrate the divine inspiration and interconnection of the Bible's contents, hence defending its legitimacy and correctness.

Despite its rich history and applications, gematria has been debated and criticised.

Some regard it as a type of superstition or manipulation, while others believe its application might lead to misinterpretation and incorrect conclusions.

The importance of gematria stems from its potential to provide a more in-depth grasp of language and the spiritual world.

Its potential uses in domains such as cryptography and code-breaking are also discussed.

Implications For Contemporary Religious And Spiritual Practices

———

The study of gematria has important ramifications for modern religious and spiritual practices.

It can, for example, provide new insights into the meaning of religious texts and symbols and help us better appreciate the mystical aspects of our religious traditions.

Furthermore, gematria can be used for personal introspection, contemplation, and connection with the divine.

However, it is critical to approach gematria with caution and humility, acknowledging its limitations and the possibility of misinterpretation.

It is also critical to avoid reducing religious and spiritual rituals to simple mathematical calculations and to preserve a holistic and balanced approach to our faith traditions.

Gematria study can help us better understand our religious and spiritual practices while strengthening our relationship with the divine.

Future Directions For Research On Gematria

———

F urther exploration of gematria's use in various cultures and religions, such as Hinduism, Chinese numerology, and Islamic numerology, are potential future paths for gematria research.   .

Continued investigation of gematria's historical evolution in Judaism and Christianity, including its employment in early Christian apologetics and influence on Christian mysticism.

Examination of the role of gematria in contemporary spiritual practices and New Age movements.

Investigation of the use of gematria in modern cryptography and code-breaking and its potential applications in other fields such as data encryption and cybersecurity.

Further exploration of gematria's theological and philosophical implications, including debates over its validity and criticisms from within religious traditions.

Study the potential psychological and cognitive effects of using gematria in spiritual and divinatory practices, including its role in promoting meaning-making, pattern recognition, and cognitive biases.

Gematria's relationship to other numerological systems, such as Pythagorean numerology and the enneagram. And where they might intersect with modern psychology and personality theory.

Notably, the use of gematria varies greatly among religious and spiritual traditions.

Some consider it a valuable tool for interpreting sacred texts and gaining deeper insights into their faith, while others view it as superstitious or even heretical.

Ultimately, it's up to individuals to discern and decide whether or not to incorporate gematria into their religious or spiritual practices.

You may or many not have heard of typology so as a little extra we will cover this next.

Gematria Verses Bible Typology

———

B ible typology and gematria are two different approaches
to interpreting the Bible.

Typology looks for patterns and symbols in the Old
Testament that prefigure or foreshadow events, people, or
teachings in the New Testament.

Gematria, on the other hand, is a method of interpreting the
numerical value of Hebrew or Greek letters and words to find
hidden meanings or connections between different passages of
Scripture.

Here are a few examples of how these two methods differ:

Noah's Ark: Typology would look at the story of Noah's Ark as
a symbol of baptism in the New Testament, with the waters of
the flood representing the waters of baptism.

On the other hand, gematria might look at the numerical value
of the letters in the word "*ark*" and find hidden meanings or
connections based on that value.

The Star of Bethlehem: Typology would see the Star of
Bethlehem as a symbol of the coming of Christ, based on the
prophecies in the Old Testament about a star that would rise
out of Jacob (**Numbers 24:17**).

Gematria might look at the numerical value of the letters in the word "*star*" and find hidden meanings or connections based on that value.

The number 666: Typology might interpret the number 666 in the book of Revelation as a symbol of the Antichrist based on the passage's context and the symbolism of the number itself. Gematria might look at the numerical value of the letters.

Typology, which draws upon the recurring themes found throughout the Bible, gives us a firmer grasp of the material at hand, in my opinion.

Typology leads us on to another related, bonus, topic which is eschatology.

Biblical Eschatology

———

The study of the end times or the final events of history as described in the Bible is known as biblical eschatology.

It delves into the end of the world and everything within it, including humanity's fate.

Believing that God's plan for the world will be fulfilled is essential for studying eschatology in the Bible.

The Bible mentions several events that will occur at the end of the world.

These include Jesus Christ's return, the final judgement of all people, the resurrection of the dead, and the construction of a new heaven and a new earth.

Christians of various denominations and intellectual backgrounds have differing perspectives on what the end times will entail. Some people adopt a literal interpretation of the events depicted in the Bible, while others take a more symbolic or metaphorical approach.

Some believe it will all happen at once, while others believe it will come gradually over time.

In whatever way it is understood, biblical eschatology is fundamental to Christian theology and a constant reminder that God ultimately controls the path of history.

Conclusion

———

This book covers a lot more than simply gematria, but I hope you liked our brief adventure together. There are more books that cover a wide range of topics that may be relevant to what you are interested in.

Before we part ways, I'd like to strongly encourage you to consider your eternal salvation on the next page.

ABCs of Salvation

———

Only Jesus Christ can save your soul and shield it from the evil one's influence.

Your next breath is not guaranteed.

The clock is ticking.

Please seek Jesus today!

The Gospel = Good News

New Testament Corinthians 15:1-4.

ABC's of SALVATION

A - ADMIT

Admit you are a sinner and have made mistakes.

Romans 3:23

B - BELIEVE

Believe that Jesus is God's Son, died on the cross for you, and rose from the grave on the third day.

Romans 10: 9-10

C - CONFESS

Confess with your mouth that Jesus is Lord of your life. Then, commit yourself to a life of following Jesus and serving others.

Romans 10:13

You WILL be saved.

Believe in Jesus Christ and have faith in his blood (*blood atonement*). Romans 3.

It is a **FREE** gift, and you do not earn it or work for it.

Thank you for reading this book. If you found it useful then please give us a thumbs-up!

Honest reviews welcome, your feedback is important to us.

About The Author

———

Anthea Peries, BSc (Hons), is a published author; she completed her undergraduate studies in several sciences, including Biology, Brain and Behaviour and Child Development.

A graduate of the British Psychological Society, she has experience in counselling and is a former senior management executive.

Anthea was born in London, and in addition to her interests in exquisite cuisine and writing, she has travelled extensively worldwide.

Giorgio is her adorable tuxedo cat who has a princely demeanour, and he is spoiled rotten but still very cute!

Resources and Useful Links

———

Https://according2prophesy.org

https://rapturekit.org

https://amirraptureready.org

https://iamawatchman.com

https://Rev310.net

savedbygrace-messiah.com/abcs-of-salvation

How to get saved:

https://youtu.be/PBfsPphGSeE

https://youtu.be/WBQPj9TeXRs

The Rapture Kit

Some Christians, anticipating that they would be raptured (*caught-up, Harpazo in Greek*) to heaven before the coming tribulation on Earth, put together what is known as "rapture kits" to ensure they are prepared for whatever may come.

The contents of a rapture kit are open to interpretation. Still, they often include the Bible, a note to loved ones back home, and some food, water, and first aid supplies.

In addition to the Bible and other religious materials, some rapture kits include money and instructions on where to meet other believers who have also been raptured.

Not all Christians subscribe to the rapture theory or the practice of storing away supplies in case it's needed.

Rather, it is a point of contention among many branches of Christianity, yet awareness of this miraculous and glorious occurrence (*Our Blessed hope*!) is nonetheless crucial.

God's punishment of the Church is not predetermined. As a result, you must take precautions to ensure that you are not left behind during the seven-year Tribulation for the House of Israel (Jacob's Trouble, Daniel's 70 Weeks), which will have global repercussions.

He will judge a Godless world.

Other Books by This Author

- *Thriving in Chaos: Practical Guide to Surviving in a World of Uncertainty. Strategies and Tools for Building Resilience, Finding Stability, and Flourishing in Turbulent Times*

- *Food Addiction*

- *Emotional Eating*

- *Sugar Cravings*

- *Night Eating Syndrome*

- *Gambling Addiction*

- *Smoking Addiction*

- *Shopping Addiction*

- *Coping with Cancer*

- *Coping with Grief*

- *Social Media Addiction*

and more.

ADDICTIONS, SUBSTANCES AND ADDICTIVE BEHAVIORS

Introduction To Addictions That People Battle Against and How to Recover

FREE E-Book:

https://digitaldome.sendibble.com/Self-Help-Books-0046c568-66201e8e

Or, https://bit.ly/3C1uiur

Honest reviews from all readers are most welcome!

Inspiring Others to Transform Their Lives

Don't miss out!

Visit the website below and you can sign up to receive emails whenever Anthea Peries publishes a new book. There's no charge and no obligation.

https://books2read.com/r/B-A-DMCG-VPBHC

BOOKS 2 READ

Connecting independent readers to independent writers.

Also by Anthea Peries

Cancer and Chemotherapy

Coping with Cancer & Chemotherapy Treatment: What You Need to Know to Get Through Chemo Sessions

Coping with Cancer: How Can You Help Someone with Cancer, Dealing with Cancer Family Member, Facing Cancer Alone, Dealing with Terminal Cancer Diagnosis, Chemotherapy Treatment & Recovery

Chemotherapy Survival Guide: Coping with Cancer & Chemotherapy Treatment Side Effects

Chemotherapy Chemo Side Effects And The Holistic Approach: Alternative, Complementary And Supplementary Proven Treatments Guide For Cancer Patients

Chemotherapy Treatment: Comforting Gift Book For Patients Coping With Cancer

Christian Books

Seeking Salvation, Secure In Belief: How To Get Sure-Fire Saved By Grace Through Faith, Rapture Ready And Heaven Bound

Thriving In Chaos: A Practical Guide To Surviving In A World Of Uncertainty: Strategies and Tools for Building Resilience, Finding Stability, and Flourishing in Turbulent Times

Divine Mathematics: Unveiling the Secrets of Gematria Exploring the Mystical & Symbolic Significance of Numerology in Jewish and Christian Traditions, & Beyond

Colon and Rectal

Bowel Cancer Screening: A Practical Guidebook For FIT (FOBT) Test, Colonoscopy & Endoscopic Resection Of Polyp Removal In The Colon

Cancer: Bowel Screening| A Simple Guide About How It Works To Help You Decide

Eating Disorders

Food Cravings: Simple Strategies to Help Deal with Craving for Sugar & Junk Food

Sugar Cravings: How to Stop Sugar Addiction & Lose Weight

The Immune System, Autoimmune Diseases & Inflammatory Conditions: Improve Immunity, Eating Disorders & Eating for Health

Food Addiction: Overcome Sugar Bingeing, Overeating on Junk Food & Night Eating Syndrome

Food Addiction: Overcoming your Addiction to Sugar, Junk Food, and Binge Eating

Food Addiction: Why You Eat to Fall Asleep and How to Overcome Night Eating Syndrome

Overcome Food Addiction: How to Overcome Food Addiction, Binge Eating and Food Cravings

Emotional Eating: Stop Emotional Eating & Develop Intuitive Eating Habits to Keep Your Weight Down

Emotional Eating: Overcoming Emotional Eating, Food Addiction and Binge Eating for Good

Eating At Night Time: Sleep Disorders, Health and Hunger Pangs: Tips On What You Can Do About It

Addiction To Food: Proven Help For Overcoming Binge Eating Compulsion And Dependence

Weight Loss: How To Not Gain Holiday Weight After Thanks Giving & Christmas Holidays Beat Post Vacation Weight Gain: Proven Ways To Jumpstart Healthy Eating

Weight Loss After Having A Baby: How To Lose Postpartum Weight After Pregnancy & Giving Birth

Food Addiction And Emotional Eating Guidebook: Proven Ways To End Binge Eating, Sugar Cravings & Eating At Night-Time

Eating Disorders: Food Addiction & Its Effects, What Can You Do If You Can't Stop Overeating?

Slim Down Sensibly: A Realistic Guide to Achieving Sustainable Weight Loss A Science-Based Approach to Healthy Eating, Exercise, and Mindset for Lasting Results

Eye Care
Glaucoma Signs And Symptoms

Food Addiction
Overcoming Food Addiction to Sugar, Junk Food. Stop Binge Eating and Bad Emotional Eating Habits

Food Addiction: Overcoming Emotional Eating, Binge Eating and Night Eating Syndrome

Weight Loss Without Dieting: 21 Easy Ways To Lose Weight
Naturally
Weight Loss Affirmations For Food Addicts: You Can Do It
Believe In Yourself Daily Positive Affirmations To Help You
Lose Weight

Grief, Bereavement, Death, Loss

Coping with Loss & Dealing with Grief: Surviving
Bereavement, Healing & Recovery After the Death of a Loved
One

How to Plan a Funeral

Coping With Grief And Heartache Of Losing A Pet: Loss Of
A Beloved Furry Companion: Easing The Pain For Those
Affected By Animal Bereavement

Grieving The Loss Of Your Baby: Coping With The
Devastation Shock And Heartbreak Of Losing A Child
Through Miscarriage, Still Birth

Loss And Grief: Treatment And Discovery Understanding
Bereavement, Moving On From Heartbreak And Despair To
Recovery

Grief: The Grieving Process, Reactions, Stages Of Grief, Risks,
Other Losses And Recovery

First Steps In The Process Of Dealing With Grief: Help for
Grieving People: A Guidebook for Coping with Loss. Pain,
Heartbreak and Sadness That Won't Go Away

Health Fitness

How To Avoid Colds and Flu Everyday Tips to Prevent or Lessen The Impact of Viruses During Winter Season
Boost Your Immune System Fast: Guide On Proven Ways For Boosting Your Immunity Against Illness And Disease.

International Cooking

Spicy Seafood Dishes: Gourmet Cooking Ideas For Curry And Spice Lovers. Introductory Guide To Decadent Seafood Cuisine With Health Benefits & Wellbeing For The Connoisseur

Noodles: Noodle Recipes Introductory Guide To Delicious Spicy Cuisine International Asian Cooking

A Taste Of Malaysia: Authentic Recipes For Nasi Lemak, Satay, Laksa, And More: Unveiling The Secrets Of Malaysian Cuisine Through Delicious And Easy-to-Follow Dishes

Discovering the Flavours and Traditions of Burma (Myanmar): A Guide to Burmese Cuisine and Culture A Journey Through Food, Fashion, Art and History

Parenting

Anger Management For Stressed-Out Parents:Skills To Help You Cope Better With Your Child

Coding Programs For Kids: Parents Guidebook: How Your Child Can Learn To Code And The Benefits For Their Future

Compassionate Collaborative Communication: How To Communicate Peacefully In A Nonviolent Way A Practical

Guide Using Effective Proven Skills For Conflict In Relationships Between Parents & Kids

Potty Training: Handbook Guide In Crap Parenting Proven Ways To Train Your Toddler Easily & Quickly With Realistic Results

Acts Of Kindness: Doing Good Deeds to Help Others

Personal Relationships

How To Talk To Your Partner: Preventing Problems Through Effective Communication In A Relationship

Quark Cheese

50 More Ways to Use Quark Low-fat Soft Cheese: The Natural Alternative When Cooking Classic Meals

Quark Cheese Recipes: 21 Delicious Breakfast Smoothie Ideas Using Quark Cheese

30 Healthy Ways to Use Quark Low-fat Soft Cheese

Introduction To Quark Cheese And 25 Recipe Suggestions: Quark Cheese Guide And Recipes

Quit Alcohol

How To Stop Drinking Alcohol: Coping With Alcoholism, Signs, Symptoms, Proven Treatment And Recovery

Relationships

The Grief Of Getting Over A Relationship Breakup: How To Accept Breaking Up With Your Ex | Advice And Tips To Move On

Coping With A Marriage Breakup: How To Get Over The Emotional Heartbreak Of A Relationship Breakdown, Signs Of Splitting Up, Divorce And Heal From A Broken Heart

Self Help

OCD: Introduction Guide Book Obsessive Compulsive Disorder And How To Recover

Sleep Disorders

Sleep Better at Night and Cure Insomnia Especially When Stressed

Standalone

Family Style Asian Cookbook: Authentic Eurasian Recipes: Traditional Anglo-Burmese & Anglo-Indian

Coping with Loss and Dealing with Grief: The Stages of Grief and 20 Simple Ways on How to Get Through the Bad Days

Coping With Grief Of A Loved One After A Suicide: Grieving The Devastation And Loss Of Someone Who Took Their Own Life. How Long Does The Heartache Last?

When A Person Goes Missing And Cannot Be Found: Coping With The Grief And Devastation, Without Losing Hope, Of When An Adult Or Child Disappears

Menopause For Women: Signs Symptoms And Treatments A Simple Guide

Remembering Me: Discover Your Memory Proven Ways To Expand & Increase It As You Get Older

Boredom: How To Overcome Feeling Bored Discover Over 100 Proven Ways To Beat Apathy

Putting Baby To Sleep: Soothe Your Newborn Baby To Sleep For Longer Stretches At Night Proven Practical Survival Guide For Tired Busy New Parents

Coping With Bullying And Cyberbullying: What Parents, Teachers, Office Managers, And Spouses Need To Know: How To Identify, Deal With And Cope With A Bully At Home, In School Or In The Workplace

Gardening For Beginners: How To Improve Mental Health, Happiness And Well Being Outdoors In The Garden: Green Finger Holistic Approach In Nature: Everything You Need To Know, Even If You Know Nothing!

Becoming Vegan For Health And The Environment: Plant Based Veganism Guidebook For Beginners: Balanced View Of The Benefits & Risks Of Being Vegetarian

Happiness & Reading Books: For Adults & Children A Proven Way To Increase Literacy Focus Improve Memory Sleep Better Relieve Stress Broaden Your Knowledge Increase Confidence Motivation & Be Happy

Caring For A Loved One With Cancer & Chemotherapy Treatment: An Easy Guide for Caregivers

Genealogy Tracing Your Roots A Comprehensive Guide To Family History Research Uncovering Your Ancestry, Building Your Family Tree And Preserving Your Heritage

Ingram Content Group UK Ltd.
Milton Keynes UK
UKHW040825030723
424469UK00004B/285

9 798215 330715